Family Portraits in Verse

Family Portraits in verse

AND OTHER ILLUSTRATED POEMS

DANIEL BROWN

Epigraph Books
Rhinebeck, New York

Paperback ISBN 978-1-954744-95-0

Library of Congress Control Number 2022920709

Book design by Colin Rolfe

Epigraph Books
22 East Market Street, Suite 304
Rhinebeck, NY 12572
(845) 876-4861
epigraphps.com

contents

DAD'S SONGS

SOME EXTRA ILLUSTRATED POEMS
(for the heck of it)

IN MEMORY OF AL SUMM

Introduction

The seeds for this book were two genealogy courses I took in the mid-80's. My parents sent me a couple of dozen family photos so I could see the family in the action of the times–doing what families do–lovers posing together, parents posing with children, posing formally and in fun.

My Dad's family were shutterbugs and many of his family photographs were taken in the early twentieth century. These include a very clear photograph of my Grandmother in 1909!!

Although the photos from my Mom's side are fewer in number, they are perhaps more expressive of the volatile lives that all families experience to one degree or another but eventually strive to overcome.

My wife Linnea Brown's family with Scandinavian immigrant roots are represented as well. They show the process and desire to assimilate through marriage, raising children and becoming American.

The cover illustration of my Aunt Virginia from the early 1940's was always a favorite. After I began to write poetry I wanted to write a verse to accompany it. I deliberated, then one morning early, (when I usually get most inspired) I realized a long thin poem was the way to go. The project took off from there. Family photos and poems began to be my near obsession.

The subjects in this book were like all of us; they were sometimes flawed, they suffered and were often unsure of themselves. They didn't know what their futures held but they lived with determination and resilience. They exhibited a sense of humor plus they were photogenic as hell. Finally they were impermanent but what they passed on is our legacy and that's the reason we respect them.

My hope is that people reading this book first of all enjoy it and secondly think and feel and appreciate the people behind your personal family images. Not just for the way their light reached a lens but for what they experienced and meant to you.

Be well one and all.

Keep reading and look for photographs and art in the world that will never be created except in your imagination.

ACKNOWLEDGMENTS

This book is dedicated to my parents

Bessie Marie Eaton Brown
April 23,1921-June 24, 2020

Daniel Warren Brown senior
April 21,1923-April 11, 2008

I'm indebted to all the ancesters who contributed to the book.
I hope I did them justice. These include.

My fraternal Grandparents:
D.Warren and Maude Rippetoe Brown

My father's siblings:
Virginia (Dinny) Brown Michlick
Catherine (Kitty) Brown Dugan
Herbert Brown

My maternal Grandparents:
Arthur and Julia Cole Eaton

My wife's Grandparents:
Sonja Pierson Kunze and Fred Kunze

Her Parents:
Rosa Kunze Winika and William A. Winika

Rosa's sister:
Sonia Kunze Karlson
William's brothers:
Wayne and Walter Winika

In addition a heartfelt thanks to all the following family and friends for their support:

Linnea Brown my beautiful and talented wife of over three decades with deep love and thanks for her contributions of advice, illustrations, writing and photos. (fredriquelinnea@gmail.com)

Lisa Winika my very talented daughter and Jill of all trades, thanks for helpful information on color and just being you.(apathwithheart23@gmail.com and Instagram lisawinika.art) **Lisa's Misunderstood Women's Project** is well worth a google search.

Jennifer Phillipson, another talented daughter who recorded and edited my public readings including those on my youtube channel **"Poetry From Shooks Pond."**

Al Summ (1944-2017) in gratitude for his love of jazz, art and 43 years of friendship.

Cynthia Winika a special thanks for gifting us with the 'Brothers" photo from 1923 (find her on Facebook or simply google her name for lots of examples of her work).

Bob Crimi for his amazing insights into jazz life in NYC during the 50's and 60's and taoism as well (bobcrimi.com)

David Watson for almost 50 years of friendship and working to maintain the legacy of Al Summ's art, as well as providing editorial assistance.

My son in law **Ted Schimdt** who was helpful with editing, encouragement and criticism.

For **Bruce Talbot and Truck Stop Record**s in Kingston, NY where the few short years of music and friendship were important beyond their time frame.

To **Coburn Library, Owego New York** for permission to use their photo of the library and for carrying on a needed tradition. (https://coburnfreelibrary.org/)

To **CAPS (Calling All Poets)** New Paltz, New York for giving me a forum for my work and inspiring me to want to become a better writer. (https://www.callingallpoets.net/)

I also want to thank the many family and friends who read and/or saw me read my work and gave encouragement and criticism:

Virginia and Julia Bauch
Stephen Brown
Liz and Tom Keating
Mike and Cindy Dale Keating
Julia and Joe Monaco
Bethany Smith

And finally a big thank you to all my Facebook friends, too many to name individually but helpful and in many cases for being friends for decades.

* * *

The art of Al Summ and the poems 'In Memory of Al Summ' and "Eubie's Hands' were previously published in **Jerry Jazz Musician.**

'Giant Morning' was previously published in a somewhat different form in **Jerry Jazz Musician.**

The poem '1958' also appeared in **Jerry Jazz Musician.**

'My Gift' was previously published in **Thema Literary Journal.**

'Hiroshima 8/5/45' was previously published in **The New Verse News.**

'The Elm Tree' appeared in a somewhat different form in **Poetic Sun Journal.**

Genealogy

A baby... (us)
            cries
mouth to breast
succored with bundled warm
arms...

Is a seedling
pollinated by yellow hovering
Mother bee

sticky with sweetness
                spreading
(family)
into a comb of birthdays

as long as... (we)
and hives exist.

Maude 1909

                Green Ivy
In a gray tone
                photo
hangs from her house
                Immaculate
as her apron is worn and
                her hair
swept up accentuating
                her smile

so much will awaken when
                she steps
off camera to follow her shadow
                the path
of this day and the future will
                evolve slowly
into a world of color where
                Ivy is green

with undertones of imagination
a stride behind her aspirations.

maude and warren 1911

She pantomimes a dance
                cane chest high, a pretend song and tap,
He flips his boater
                sharing a joke like a vaudeville comic,
she looks at him with the laughing abandon of first
love, he's so sure of her applause.
In an ankle length white dress and straw hat they'll
never step forward from the oval frame.
She will feel loss in the coming war
                cancer will ravage him in future decades;
        together they will share a life of place and family
            posed for all time on this innocent summer day
seven night stars will never show the way.

Danny was so mean

Turn over Photo One:
(In Grandmother's hand)

"I took these when
it was not very light.
And Danny was so mean
he kept
trying

       to

          get

             a

            way".

And Danny does fade
as Einstein's relativity
finds him almost invisible
as his energy + mischief = light
that won't stand still
or listen to reason.

Turn over Photo Two: (in Dad's hand)

" Din & Kitty &
and I"
posed politely as
Danny's experiments
in the effect of
disbursement of light
on parental authority

is checked by a
cautionary hand on his shoulder,
Din and Kitty (in their
wonderful winter hats)

are at the precise axis of maturity
between suppressing a smile at
Danny's quantum antics
and understanding the serious responsibility
of family togetherness.

Portrait
of Virginia

(EARLY FORTIES)

She stands
as tall
as oak
with twin
maples shooting
vertical left
and right
her head
balanced near
the peak
of the
house across
the street.
Her forties
skirt reaching
below her
knees portrays
her elongated
beyond reality
taller than
life when
in fact
she was
sixty inches
stocking feet.
Consider this
illusion and
sideward smile
equaled her

sense of
self which
was as
two storied
as any
house on
the street.

Herbert with the Ball

Inscribed on the back:
"Mother in the backyard looking at the flowers, Herbert with the ball". Did they stage it? Did Herbert jump with the ball in the glove? The simple joy of the thing makes me want it to be real, an action shot with an old camera, one chance in a hundred, at least. Those I could ask are gone, one of those questions you never think to ask when someones alive. A greater question perhaps is grandmother's flowers, the second kind of miracle within the frame. Her attention was so different from Herbert on the other side of the yard, his feet suspended in air. She's so casually focused on floral balance and color he and my father probably walked by day after day without noticing. I've driven by that house and saw the patch of lawn where the ball was caught, the jump was made, whether staged or not and as I age I think about where Grandmother's flower bed rested just out of rolling distance of an escaping ball. When Herbert died at 92, I gave the photo to my cousin who had never seen it and she placed it in a frame and put it in a special place. Two remaining views of an afternoon.

two universes
a flower bed
a perfect catch

nine short poems and epilogue for my father
(THANKS FOR THE IDEA WALLACE)

1.How strange their
cross referenced birthdays:
Dad April 21, 1923
Mom April 23, 1921.
What could push a couple
toward marriage, the desire
to belong and share bodies
and family more than this
fortuitous gem of commonality?
Nothing!! This is so coincidental
it shivers the spine and makes
you gasp at their willingness to
close their eyes and
swan dive into deep turbulent water
because the sirens rolled
a winning seven and sang like
The Andrews Sisters.

2. Look out...
...suddenly whooping
 he'd belt out
"Streets of Laredo" or "Danny Boy"--

(deep within the kernel of lyrics;
he felt the dying Cowboy's lament

The lonely visit to a grave
sleeping through seasons,

the tangled red rose and
black briar knot of "Barbara Allen";

he tried to explain to his children
who laughed or didn't understand,

there's a certain loneliness
in interests unshared)

and then as the mood struck
an impromptu
click heeled little jig

all the while
perfectly sober he was.

3. On this day/ on this day
each year on memorial day/
he bugled taps/ across the river
day is done.

4. Sunday backroads
rear windows barely cracked for air

interminate complaints
of breeze on the back of his neck

a dinner of plain cheese pizza
and humid melting ice cream to come

two quiet parents, animated chatter
among four sweaty sardined siblings

Dad guides the chevy home
to the narrow evening street

crushed in by houses
muscling too close for twelve arms to reach

another seven safe timetables roll in
like a fog cloudbank low from the hillside

sunlight is veiled yet still will shine.

5. He cupped
reservoirs of water
in his hands
and watched
it trickle through
his fingers.

6. When grinning saturday night cars devoured trees
   and discarded their drivers
like candy wrappers— or those in disarrayed night
   clothes clutched cold bathroom tiles—
he left interrupted dreams to ferry them to antiseptic
hospital or morgue. Then on monday morning a
   filthy decade
of factory work would pass, breathing in chemicals,
   trudging on.

7. 1958

(Illustration by Linnea Brown)

His old records spun,
                        the needle
dropped,

Hiss, Hiss, Hiss
Clickety, Click, Clickety, Click

78 times 60
too fast to read the label.

Innocent ears
spellbound by Satchmo's cornet

(Muskat Ramble and Struttin'
With Some Barbecue)

                          heard
at the speed of sight and sound.

Surface noise, such imperfection
a window opening...
                    to a way of life.

8. Awakened
from cancer   (3x) with
                    exhumed trust and love
(guardedly) cared for by his wife (my mother)
who emerged from
                    second hand efficiency
to finally soothe and comfort (resolved to resume)

                              as if their
partnership vows had happened
only
the
day
before.

1929

9. During his last days/ a spoken half-memory/
"It wasn't me, Mother".
A secret of childhood---exhaled
                    At last.

Epilogue:
Buried in dust
With his infant daughter

Sleeping together
Ornate clay vessels
Never filled

In heaven (of the
Mind's eye)

The cemetery dirge
Is finished

Now a joyous
And welcoming
Parade.

MOTHER AND CHILD

Reflect on 1950, Mother joyfully holds her
son

fragile and unaware of the great fear his early arrival
birthed,

or the early arrival 1949 of the baby named, never
cradled

or her tragic flood of anticipation after this great
wheel came
undone

water that spans the belly may be gathering dark
thunder

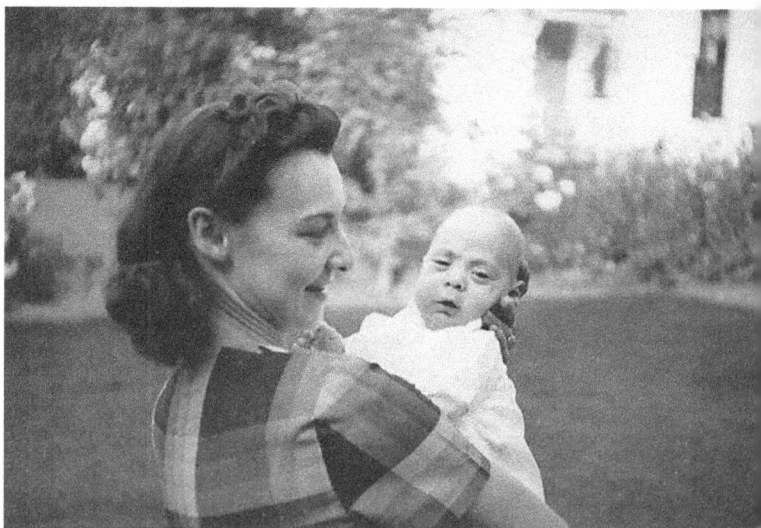

the body may erupt before soft rain returns for small
blue walkway
flowers:
how
large now if
he rested in
her arms

their seasoned
hands

forgotten
clouds of
acceptance...

as curved and tired
she ambles each evening
toward her small bed
in soft pink slippers
at 8:00 p.m.

MY GIFT
THE OLD FAMILY STONE
"INFANT DAUGHTER OF
DANIEL & BESSIE BROWN
1949–1949"

Her features are more like Dad's side of the family;
Red hair, now white, cut short, combed back Mary
    Astor style.
She likes old movies, also The Everly's,
Thelonious Monk and Bach.
She's worked in bookstores and record stores,
has married now with a family.
I'm inside the mirror with her all the time,
Silent by her shoulder.

She's become a poet and reads regularly in a college
    town art gallery.
Tonight she's reading a poem, a psalm to a brother
    that doesn't exist,
Though she knows and understands,
Then I step from the mirror and she steps in,
We crisscross like a prisoner swap and it's I with her
    by my shoulder.
I read a poem for her and her secret breath in my
    lungs.

1949 Sister Virginia you gave up everything for my
    arrival 1950.
1949 Sister Virginia my perennial birthday gift.
1949 Sister Virginia my legacy.
1949 Sister Virginia with deepest thanks.

Whatever I am, doing well or slumped in failure,
I couldn't have done it without you, kiddo.
You always had my back.
We've been a fine team all along, as if we had,
In reality been able to race our bikes down the little
  hill,
Around the corner, heading home,
On a humid July afternoon killing time,
Just before dinner in, let's say, oh, 1960.

Arthur and Julia in uniform

                                 In hospital uniforms
the proud camera lens held them close
                             hemmed like congested
TB sufferers they served
                                 formally posed
from shoe to headpiece in
                                costumes of love
toward the bequeathed
                           future a similitude that
changed with nakedness
                              when starched body
touch brought forth children
                                 like constrained
lungs coughing forth a
                             future that unraveled
into garments of
                                 woven silica dust.

Four Generations 1919
(PROSE POEM WITH CINQUAIN)

My Mothers older sister was held by her mother, her father next to her, upright and proud, her grandparents on either side. He has a dapper mustache and bowtie, she stood, shoulders back, arms crossed, wise Irish face stern with just a twinkle of a smile hidden for the camera.

Her great grandparents sat in front so fragile, dry corn stalks long past seed resting in clumps of spent soil. It occurs to me that they– my great-great grandparents, shallow cheeked and gaunt, about 1860, as young people, made love, naked and began a family. Their faces became my Mother's face as hers became mine. Faces that existed before me and will beyond, like the sun in a morning mirror outside the window each day.

faces
old, young, here, gone
a changing hologram,
as I stroll my life, they become
as one.

julia's Face

The zen masters ask:
what was your face
before you were born?
it was Julia's face
the eyes and mouth
of generations of daughters,
intersticed tributaries who feel
her warm reflection
on their faces
when they smile
a formal thin mouth
or wide in laughter
no one else but Julia
as she was.
 (is).

the eaton sisters
(CIRCA 1927)

In identical lace dresses

I imagine are yellow
delicate in black patent shoes
and brown bobbed hair
posed as innocently
as the bouquet of flowers
witnessing from the side table
three sisters dressed
in lace yellow dresses
a triangle as close as aperture allows

with a sudden disruption
in a another years time

their postures
will heave
from the frame
shatter like glass
when the fourth sister crowns
released by the passing of Mother
which they will just quite remember
the rest of their lives.

GranDFaTHer's asHes

What should we do with the ashes?
His remains, now that the grandfather
we barely knew is remembered;
these are questions of a ten year old
who didn't know the visitor who arrived one day
and hugged our Mother, sat on the couch and talked
like a long lost friend. In one old photo, shirt off,
skin weathered like leather, hands
gnarled and splintered as he stood near his house
which existed somewhere I didn't know. He was
always working, unclothed from the waist up--
    climbing high
ladders to fix gutters or the roof-- crouched low to
    the ground
tending plants-- always fixing, repairing, planting,
    mulching,
as if he rested the destructive past,
the reeling incoherent anger of the past,
the official decrees of the past might immure re-
    demption.

What should we do with the ashes of the half
    clothed redeemer
in the old beat up photo who restored and secured
    and tended
and did what he could to reunite with his children
    and grandchildren,
not always sure who he was. The Doctors told him
    to slow down.

Mother knew he wouldn't. He needed the work,
    needed the process,
keeping busy as if one nail, one vegetable at a time
would finally tip the scales like a wheelbarrow
    dumping bricks.
What should we do with his ashes?
Will his remains live within us, when our leathered
    grandfather,
almost invisible, is no longer remembered?

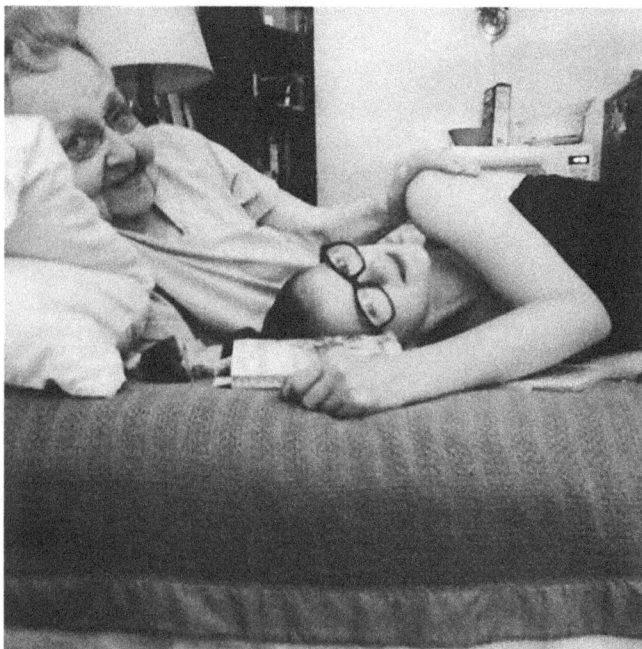

(photograph courtesy Julia Bauch)

MOM WITH THE GIRLS
(FOR ALL THE GIRLS SHE LOVED)

She seemed to walk in past shadows
the distant cold moon
over her shoulder

not so: with the girls
her smile was an immediate
offering of hope

they were her: these young women
beginning their walk
into dawn

they were her: despite every endurance
tomorrow's gift
was a gracious candle

melted from waxed moon cycles,
gifted by her own women, ashes in embers,
sunrise passed from one hand to another.

young sonja
(SWEDISH VOCATIONAL SCHOOL CIRCA 1906)

1. Their education:
domestication of girls
learning service trades
for the new world.
Grandmother sat with
the dreamers, sewing threads
of Sven America, to a land of
stitched alliances and
butter cream where
blistered hands and Sonja's
hopeful eyes were
her nervous ticket to
Ellis Island.

2. The lines were forgotten over time,
Sonja's gurgling stomach
and high starched collar
brought her one step closer to the
Manhattan gang plank,
to an agency to find work--
upstate, cooking, cleaning
marriage, children,
tidy decades swept away
as Grandmother, with work- a- day
smile, caught in a brief moment of rest
threw out strange
sounding Swedish words
for the delight of Grandchildren.

(photo by Linnea Brown nee Winika circa 1962)

Rosa the First Born

The first spring flower
a patulous
ripening of dreams

Mama and Papa hold her
as a small seed
first born

daughter
of Scandinavia
and America

white blossoms
will drop each year
under the native dogwood

future seasons
of roses that named her
will bear

boughs spanning
Norse stars
reflecting over the Hudson.

THE KUNZE SISTERS
(EARLY 1920s)

Looking from the the cracked frame
their monochrome countenance
is the story

--the balance of children
and families

Rosa you never
failed to smile, cameras
were great friends

Sonia a child of
surprise wide eyed
hesitant unsure

with blonde hair ribbons and reactions
you became through birth

in matching dresses
two hemispheres of mother

who stood proudly
behind you.

THE KUNZE SISTERS
(CIRCA EARLY 1930S)
(LINKED RENGAY VERSE WITH **LINNEA BROWN**)

How does
light form images
from small moments

> **two sisters hands at sides**
> **evolved from seeds before them**

Rosa's smile, Sonia's casualness
were scattered
by white bird wings spread in flight

> **do simple elements**
> **reap something great from**
> **ordinary life**

birds crest into a journey
that fan feathers of light

> **until touching down**
> **on paper**
> **a moment captured.**

Brothers (9/1/23)
(FOR CYNTHIA WINIKA AND LINNEA
BROWN)

–Wool flat caps
buttoned collars
tight to the chin

for a warm late summer outing
left with autumn dusk, 1923
–not brothers laughing

in boats–
boats that drift life
from one point to

another–
water following
it's special path

ignoring cameras
that blink for a second
at three brother's laughing–

–resting
on a piano
a century later.

45

DaD'S SONGS

HE SURE LIKED TO SING

(In my Mind Like A Cacophony
of Charles Ives Parades)*

* In 1912 the composer Charles Ives wrote the Fourth Of July movement to his Holiday Symphony. In it he portrays the pandemonium of two marching bands converging on the town square in Danbury Connecticut in the 1880's.

Even though his record collection contained mostly big band, jazz and a smattering of blues, my Dad loved to sing folk songs, many that he must have learned as a kid from my Grandparents or heard on the radio. With him in mind, I've selected a few that were among his favorites to adapt as poems.

If the words to the songs are not familiar to you they are a google search away. Keep in mind that being folk songs, there are multiple versions to many of the lyrics.

A note on 'Froggie Went A Courtin':
"According to Albert Jack in his book "Pop Goes the Weasel, The Secret Meanings of Nursery Rhymes" (pp. 33–37, copyright 2008), the earliest known version of the song was published in 1549 as "The Frog Came to the Myl Dur" in Robert Wedderburn's "Complaynt of Scotland". He states that in 1547 the Scottish Queen Consort, Mary of Guise, under attack from Henry VIII, sought to marry her daughter Princess Mary (later Mary Queen of Scots), "Miss Mouse", to the three-year old French Prince Louis, the "frog". The song resurfaced a few years later, with changes, when another French (frog) wooing caused concern—that of the Duke of Anjou and Queen Elizabeth I in 1579. Elizabeth even nicknamed Anjou, her favorite suitor, "the frog".

1. WRECK OF THE OLD 97
(DISASTER OF THE FAST MAIL TRAIN)

Got my orders in Monroe, Va.
47 minutes behind schedule
can't keep the mail waitin'
we got a guv'ment contract
push it... Boy ... push it.. that's an order, son!!
Fireman just keep her stokin', don't let up now--
going 90 miles an hour--
down the Danville grade-- can't slow down--
the throttle valves stuck-- can't hold the pressure--
won't make the curve--
flying off the trestle
THE SCALDING STEAM!!
(when I'm found have mercy for a poor engineer)
near er my go d t o th e ee e

2. Barbara Allen
(DEDICATED TO LISA WINIKA AND HER
MISUNDERSTOOD WOMEN'S PROJECT)

Oh, Barbara,
What did you say? In the green swelling month of
   May,
famous last words, "young man I think you're
   dying".

Sweet William, dying in remorse, (read cancer)
sends his man servant (William's rich we presume)
to Barbara's town (across the tracks).

142   POPULAR SONGS.

BARBARA ALLAN

It fell about the Martinmas day,
   When the green leaves where falling,
Sir James the Graham in the west country,
   Fell in love with Barbara Allan.

She was a fair and comely maid,
   And a maid nigh to his dwelling,
Which made him to admire the more,
   The beauty of Barbara Allan.

She comes to him slowly, slowly
like seething red kindling ash
and says what she says, as he turns away.

She reminds Sweet William, not so sweet
of drinking a conceited toast to ladies fair
though none for her as she stood mocked and
    scorned.

Barbara's a conquest of Sweet Will, possibly
    pregnant
(twas' May with green buds swellin', afterall) in one
    version
she warns virgins to watch out for Sweet Williams'
    on the prowl.

Turning his face to the wall in shame
he bids adieu and asks for kindness
for Barbara Allen.

The tolling church bells call her "hard" (bong)
    "hearted" (bong bong)
and her rage, justified with no outlet, not leavened
    by the ages
or expressed in feminist groups turns to remorse.

She then dies of a broken heart-- the common cold
    of folk songs--
though it's more likely suicide
all the pain outside the frame of simple lyrics is
    buried deep within it.

In one rendering Barbara is buried in the "new"
    church yard,
aha, definitely ahead of her time, and Sweet William
    in the "old" one,
his sense of entitlement has hardly changed but
    because of Barbara shifted.

"Oh, I wish I hadn't" sing Barbara and William
The lament that pumps through all our hearts
entwines both the rose and briar growing from their
    graves
until they climb the church wall to the top
and can climb no further.

3. Froggie went a' courtin'
(HE DID RIDE)

Here he rides, an absurd little amphibian
a frog ridin'-- cartin' a sword and pistol,
like some sort of official figure, a long
forgotten duke or a current corrupt cop,
pompous and filled with his position and power in
   life,
askin' to marry demure Miss Mouse.
She must ask permission from her Uncle Rat
who has control, financial, political, sexual over a
   vast
network of grain silos and empty attics.
Rat after meeting with his untidy cabinet
among chewed wire and acorn shells
sees the political advantage of bringing the kingdom
of frog and rodent together as leverage
against the growing power of bats and barn owls.
Marriage and control over territory against other
territory, the old lily pad pond in alliance
with the kingdom of hidden passages
and household kitchen scraps.
Such a tenuous wedding and grand scheme
for a pond where an absurd little amphibian
ridin' with miniature weapons can be ripped asunder
by any cruel schoolboy while his mouse bride may
lay dead with a bloated stomach
at any time after ingestin' poison in the pantry.
Not to mention the shady back alley doublecrosses
and vying for power of various toads, moles and
   groundhogs.

Best laid plans of frogs, mice, rats
and bestial human aristocracy destroyed
by desire for dominion and sovereignty far past
  reason.

A children's song, yes, and so much more.

4. Danny BOY

The far pipes are calling
To Danny, a son or husband
off to war, or America
to start over.

The death pipes are calling
to a Father, a Mother
a bride who must stay
as Danny
goes.

Summer is gone
rose petals fall
Danny departs, death stays,
pipes echo across glens
calling for leaving
calling to stay
calling for loss

death stays below
the hushed white snow
in summer sun
in autumn shadows

knowing Danny will return
as sure as Mother, Father,
or bride remain, casting
a never ending survey of
the hushed mountainside
below.

5. THE Prisoner's Song

If we all had wings of angels
over each prison wall
we would
fly

oh, we would
meet each other
in the
moonlight

and the
red winged
moon

would nestle us
forever in
freedom.

6. STREETS OF LAREDO

A shootout.
Over a whore at Rosie's
or a card game,
a young cowboy, likely drunk
lays in the street wrapped
in white cold clay linen.

"Please stranger
hear my sad story
you're a cowboy
you'll understand:
won't you? I done wrong
shot in the chest, going to die".

What of the shooter?
Still whorin' at Rosie's
or at the card house
any remorse or justice for
starting a national legacy
of guns solving arguments,

that drums beating
the slow death march,
being buried in green valley sod,
won't change, that roses tossed on the coffin
by equine comrades, centaurs of the10 gallon hat
won't deaden the thud of
a cold linen death for just "doing wrong".

7. MOLLY MALONE

Poor sweet Molly pushing the wheelbarrow
always onward-- chanting-- crying "Cockles and
    mussels, alive, alive, oh",
always pushing onward-- as her entire family, father
    and mother,
fishmongers all,
had pushed--onward-- everyone, every generation,
the sad chant, the cry "Cockles and mussels, alive,
    alive, oh",
through each Dublin street broad and narrow life
    after life
hemmed in on wet cobbled stone streets
until even the fever-- the consumption-- couldn't
stop her onward chant and pushing-- Molly's ghost
    cry
never ending" Cockles and mussels, alive, alive, oh".
even in death.

some extra ILLUSTRATED poems

(FOR THE HECK OF IT)

In which
Other forms
From spiders to elm limbs
Become extended family
By choice..

(illustration by Linnea Brown)

Garden Buddha

—Nothing but a
collection of molecules
which science tell us
don't even touch

—a bit of algae
on the third eye
where sun doesn't
settle

—all the features
beatific smile
beggar bowl hands and lotus
asana resemble form

because our senses say so—
what do they know
about spiders
touching down

on his illusory shoulder
spinning silk
like iron among
ancient dust—.

walt whitman

My taste in poetry generally runs to short forms with economic language. Walt Whitman is one of the poets who's an exception. His numerations and compassion for all people, places and nature continue to influence contemporary poetry, including this small tribute.

So this poem is dedicated to the great American orator, whose gray beard pointed to love in so many directions.

Part 1 is based on part 11 of 'Song Of Myself'
Part 2 is based on 'Crossing Brooklyn Ferry'
Part 3 is based on various sections of 'The Wound Dresser'

(illustration by Linnea Brown)

1. With smiling eyes and whiskers   shaking so
   very lightly
                    Walt   squatting
                      on his   haunches
---leisurely scratching the brambles on his back---
watches young men naked   laughing   splashing
a brigade of 27 in an afternoon pond   blue into
   green into wet fun
floating on their backs---- reporting for duty only to
   the sun   belly up
to the light   holding no shields for protection
   only floating---
the sun will soon set and make the sputtering beard
   water
muted rays of laughter.
     With smiling eyes of love and distance
     he   crosses and crawls   quietly   to
an old house on the rise mannered and needing
   paint and repair
and peers   in the window   a maid   twice their
   age
watches the young men--- the room is dark   she
   breathes
aged dry dust from brocaded curtains   while her
   fingers
gently caress the pleats of her dress.
They are all men unfamiliar but in her loneliness
splashes with them now   unseen   naked and
   unashamed.
     Walt smiles as he watches:
                    (He is her desire
                     He is her house
                     He is her eyes
                     He is her breath)
                  (She is his compassion.)

2. His gray beard points the way;
down the length of Fulton Street
to the Brooklyn Ferry, Walt opens his lungs
like wings, flying into him instantly deeply,
deeply, he inhales images, myriads of them
and exhales page after page of transcendent verse.
He feels the living sound of things
unmoving except for empty hustle
and dust. The entirety of Fulton street on this day
is his--- valuable, temporary, then lost. It enters his
pores.
The skyscrapers of Brooklyn and New York,
people coming and going on busy sidewalks--
in ordinary fashion, starched collars, bustles and
parasols with no
skin showing not even an unlaced ankle. And
ordinary faces
and fashion of generations unborn, hurrying to work
or home.
Fathoms of oily water and wharf,
seagulls circling over the currents as a congregation
fighting for crusts of redemption bread.
Walt sees and loves it all.
As he steps aboard the ferry, it sinks low in the
water
from the weight of visions beneath his old slouch
hat.

3. Would scalpels cease
if the cannons were silent?
Would I still kill
if my arm remained?
Ruined at Fredericksburg
I breath fevered questions
in a Washington infirmary.
My cot is a raft of blood.

The orderly Walt
brings sweet oranges and poems.
He visits boys row after row
With rolled white bandages
and black red covered notebooks
to write letters home.
There is no more perfect place
for him I believe. He sings a poem now.
We share silent harmony to what must be.

I feel my eyes are drowning.
I'm driftwood floating away
to a pond far from war
to join a regiment of 27 in the afternoon heat.
Ripples of laughter from each comrade
spread circles that begin and end nowhere.

In our nakedness and freedom we're watched over
by the joyous yearning eyes of both Maid and Poet
arm in arm, through lonely dust covered windows
on the hill
unseen from below.

Linnea in Bamboo

Hollow
bamboo shoots surround her

absolute grace touches her
radiant smile

if one were
to factory them into a farm of flutes

there would be no greater sound
than her silence.

(photograph by Jennifer Phillipson)

Family Portraits in Verse

small town librarian

Her house was near
the library so
she never had far to walk.
She stepped softly
among the shelves,
our avian Mother Artemis
of the card catalog
and dewey decimal system.
Each day she secretly shared
along with books she loaned
the librarians creed:
ideas just beyond your reach
guide you toward a question.
The arbitrators of small town morality
who censured
the life out of curiosity
with a wagging finger
barely knew she existed
or what she represented
if they had
they would have screeched
like blind old owls
in the steeple.
She continued stamping cards
and setting due dates
such ordinary behavior–
while in turn, allofeeding fledglings–
such a quiet act of freedom.

LIMITATIONS
(IN MEMORY OF BELVA LOCKWOOD)

"heaven and earth have their limitations yet the
    seasons return"
                                            I Ching
    Book of Changes

Outside your window

the Susquehanna curves the bend
                    You: the turning current of seasons

presidential runs doomed to ridicule

decades before your sisters hard won suffrage
                    You: sagacious knitter
of folly

shuttle in your hands

                    You: the weft

that altered the thread of a river

which spun and thrashed

and changed the weave of oceans.

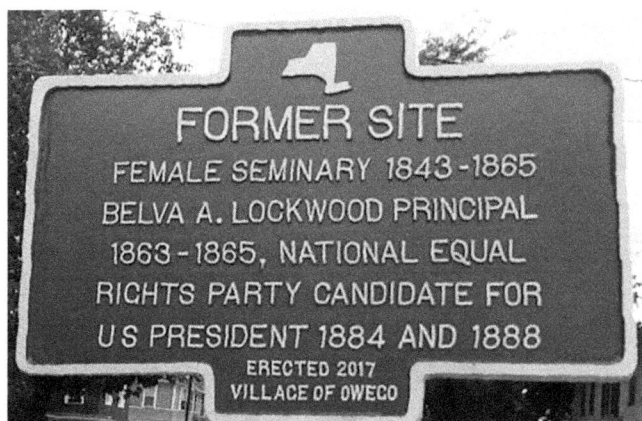

FORMER SITE
FEMALE SEMINARY 1843-1865
BELVA A. LOCKWOOD PRINCIPAL
1863-1865, NATIONAL EQUAL
RIGHTS PARTY CANDIDATE FOR
U S PRESIDENT 1884 AND 1888
ERECTED 2017
VILLAGE OF OWEGO

HIROSHIMA 8/5/1945

Glowing morning busy sidewalks

children playing or in carriages
a buzz in the sky

giant mosquito
a moment later
cinder and ash.

(Unknown photographer, digital tinkering by the author)

THE ELM TREE

Each

morning

the

old elm's branch

curves

like a wave

in a Japanese print

held in balance

before

foaming

as

surf.

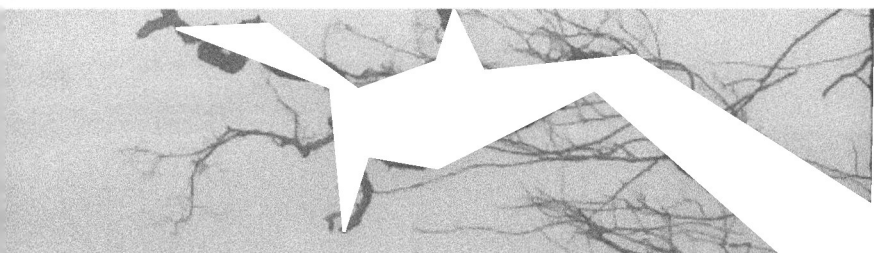

(original photo Linnea Brown with digital alteration by the author)

Man Walking with a Staff
(AFTER THE PAINTING BY SHEN ZHOU
1427–1509)

He's in there somewhere
old tiny insect, everythings so massive
around him, above and below
a loose boulder
could crush him like a fly

-- he expects nothing
only to journey the mountain path
on fragile cricket legs
until he reaches the summit
that patiently waits his joyful haiku --

perhaps he will be brushed aside
by a slippery stone or weariness
allowing him to go no further
--these matters are not his decision
neither failure or triumph

only one foot
in front
of
the
other as

he passes
a snail
wriggling back down
singing a droning mantra
to the morning.

IN MEMORY
OF AL SUMM

Al Summ (1944-2017) never tired of
preaching jazz to the world.

I learned about jazz music like a
student with my guru as did many
others.

His paintings and drawings show
a great love for jazz music and its
creators.

in memory of al summ

Now. Lowered into
sacred earth where
Monk, Miles, Coltrane,
Pres and Billie dwell.

Where Dodo Marmarosa
isn't alive and well
and Bird doesn't live.

Where all the butterfly notes
that Bill Evans and Don Friedman played
are their restful cushions. Now.

Now. Listen to the earth's holy universal
Bebop vibration
beyond time
beyond space
beyond. Now.

BELIEVING

Bill Evans
(three years before his final season)
plays 'You must believe in Spring'
sadly
as if he doesn't believe
(wait----)
a slight up tempo
(maybe)?
then Eddie Gomez's bass solo
and piano refrain.
(Yes, of course, bursting flowers
through snow,
why not?)

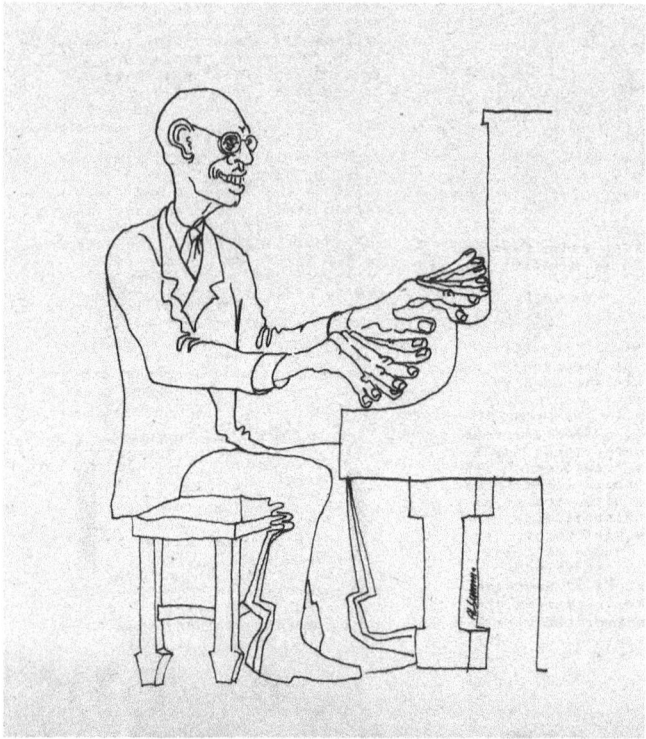

EUBIE'S HANDS
(FOR EUBIE BLAKE)

They stretched octaves
across the sheet music
and the decades
of "Charleston Rag"
fingers like twisted bent tree trunks
remembered rivers of antiquity
flowed through his veins.

There were about a million
of them when he got going,
playing good old shuffle along
white teeth ragtime
for broadway dicty uptown folks,
as he secretly with a left hand
as uniform as early morning
chorus lines
tapping,

sat in bemused silence
and ageless joy
peeking over his glasses
with swollen tree trunk fingers
and currents of cerise creation that
slowly stripped the buffoon clown mask
varnish from America's face
and painted a portrait of slow rising freedom,
hardly noticed over time,
that America can't look away from
(although it tries)
much less ever diminish.

ETERNAL-LEE
(FOR LEE KONITZ)

**Preface: "In Taoism "Wu Wei" is a concept
Meaning natural action or action without struggle,
An alignment with the flow of life".**

Each song was a search inside
Outward toward a new dimension.

Lee experimented, composed, changed,
Exalted with fingers, breath,
And mind a new way to hear the
American Songbook.
Seventy years, seventy million
Alto sax improvisations,
Endless process and
Fluid sound sculptures,
Not notated in the original score
Or sung on the Broadway Stage.

Like Michaelangelo knew the body of
David existed in the stone before being released
Or as Zen Monks reach satori by understanding
The true nature of grains of sand or snails
Climbing Mt.Fuji slowly, slowly.
All things sing together. Always.
He was the song.
Each chorus,
Each gig, each decade, a surprise.
Transition.

'All The Things You Are'
                    Became 'Ablution'
A cleansing of the past toward a a tradition
Of freedom.

'Body And Soul'
                    Became 'Figure and Spirit'
A dream dance, an ethereal ballad
Deep inside, molded intuitively,
Sent into the world with grace and style.

'What Is This Thing Called Love'
                    Became 'Subconscious-Lee'
Freudian pun and ongoing childhood
Question: Love is what?

From forties big bands and Miles Davis' 'Birth Of
   The Cool'
Until the virus of 2020, Lee turned jazz
Into himself, and himself into jazz.
From the past
To beyond, within to without, up to down, all the
   way around,
Played straight on a course or veering into free jazz
   excursions.
All the same, all to expand the
Familiar. Student and teacher both.
With enjoyment and love.

In his last years, like an seasoned professor,
Lee would talk to his audience
About the songs he played and the way
He and jazz altered them.

He knew that beyond
His life the body of song must
Continue to be released from stone
To climb, slowly, slowly up
Mountain paths toward the summit
For as long as it takes, which is
Of course, Eternal-Lee.

Giant Morning

In the warm morning sun
I listen to John Coltrane play
"Giant Steps"

nature seems to agree
garden weathervanes spin
wood and metal wind chimes
tap a delicate kalimba background

thousands of boughs absorb
overlapping descending sheets
of sunlight shifting
in the breeze

casting flickering
modulating rays
waves of light and dark
in harmony

shimmering as fast as Coltrane's scales
a spectrum of sound and sight
upon the ear of earth.

ALBERT STINSON (1944–1969)

Who were you? Up and
coming 1960's bass man,
Heroin and OD smack have

Erased you. So few
record gigs. And live dates, some
hard core fans can't forget.

ALBERT STINSON:

Answer me this; when
you were dying did
did your bass beg in anguish

knowing there would be
no answer for ruined de-
votion? So that this portrait,

pencil and shadow
blesses one more sad
silent needle memorial.

End Note

They stand In morning fog
outlines barely recognizable
as forms of myself
arriving from hometowns
north and south

as far flung as gray/blue Civil War

perhaps dark beer jazz bars
every note a conversation waiting

why not Japan home of Zen and Haiku
each common relative
past and future walking their path

DESPITE COLOR OR CONTINENT
GUIDING US
THEN FADING.

ABOUT THE AUTHOR

Daniel Brown was brought up in Owego, NY and moved to the Hudson Valley in 1972.

At age 58 following the death of his Father and finding more years in the past than in the future he began to write poetry. Over the next few years, poetry became a daily process and a life work he needed to pursue. Daniel has been published in Chronogram magazine, the online journals and blogs Ekphrastic Review, MONO, Jerry Jazz Musician, Poetic Sun and print anthologies published by THEMA literary journal, the Haiku Society of America, MONO anthology #3, and MIGHTIER: Poets For Social Justice. Daniel is appreciative and happy every time his work is accepted. He has hosted a youtube channel "**Poetry From Shooks Pond**" and lives in Red Hook, New York with his wife, daughter and two cats.

www.ingramcontent.com/pod-product-compliance
Lightning Source LLC
Chambersburg PA
CBHW022035090426
42741CB00007B/1070